I0753820

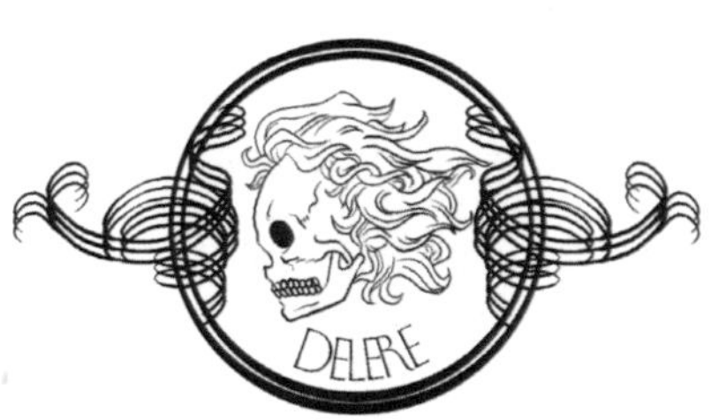
DELERE

First Published In 2014 by
Delere Press LLP

~

Photography: Marilyn Goh
Graphic Design: Joanne Pang

~

Delere Press LLP
Block 370G Alexandra Road
#09-09 Singapore 159960

www.delerepress.com

~

Delere Press LLP Reg No.
T11ll1061k
ISBN 978-981-11-4172-0

A Perfect Sphere On A Frictionless Plane

poems by

Dustin Hellberg

Dedication

~

For Trish, because I said I would.

For Jake Hayes. You're missed, brother.

And to the loving memory of my Mother.

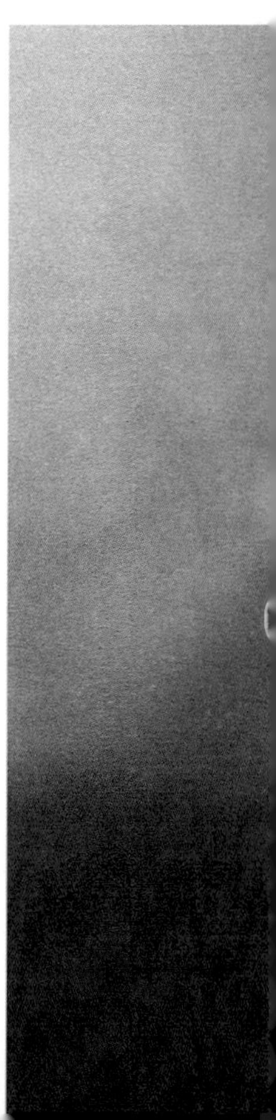

Centripetal,
Centrifugal:

Fugue, and petal.

—Ronald Johnson

~ Contents ~

SPHERE

~ Contents ~

PLANE

SPHERE

No crude bid, I hope, to ponder the answer
to the merest question formed when, squat,
you pissed in the train tunnel, no chance for
privacy as I snapped the joking photo. And what

then of the bitumen tide that beats boulders
into rhetorical granules, deep in sea-pockets,
or that near-invisible hunch of your shoulders
when tired and pressed you paused in that socket

of dark stones which suddenly, coldly flashed
with surprising fury, like a phoenix or anvil
blasting sparks? No... simply two people, cached
and alone in one moment's glimmer, who strolled

below the mountain's lazarine starkness,
while around them wheeled in startled flight
an ancient machinery of light and darkness,
and another of darkness and light.

Cinque Terre

Subpoena

Floodlights and right angles govern the scene
from the roof above the town's one park, above people
wearing photos of their faces over their own,
whose movements are just a motion in air,
who are beautiful in this keening peace,
who empty bottle after bottle, their heart
beating an inebriate dance in rarified halls,
each mouth a vote, each breath an exile stalled
between the past and the cold click of teeth,
the church and steeple, the fall and the grace.
And where is that woman I'd have built a house for, of wattles
and mud, except for my kiss of asphalt, except this evening
failing to erase her elemental kisses which dropped like morphine
and manna once, while the moon fell like a leper's rattle?

Mortal and bewildered we hit the ground,
hoping not to shatter these heads and hands of clay.
If there were just one way to misquote the sky,
or quiet or poverty it can only be with tongue
when the vacuum fills with fire and the blinds are napalm
smeared over this book and this ashtray
where I can talk of sadness in my undershirt
because of the way I would have ravished
you, mortal and bewildered, you with the dirt
beneath your fingernails, whose throat like a psalm
pretended to know me, and lay its raphaeline
arc across my pillow sometimes. But this is not
an issue of faith, of desire postponed or forgot,
for those in this mind of smoke and terrorists' dreams.

There is a space so expositive, so clear
that we must be careful what we put
in it, which in this way it resembles the boot
my father's father wore in Korea
filling with blood, the way history fills space,
when it is not sleeping. It does not even seem
to breathe while it is sleeping. Shot and left, he
crawled the miles back, and drank water from a stream
with a helmet he'd found a man's head in. Season,
take it back in now, little lamp against the dark,
held out at arm's length against the vespers
of drink in this drug-and-hoodlum-run park
where the cracked-tin lips bleed and whisper
to a ministry of animal, quake and seizure.

Stylus

Edgewater breakwater
Impossible tendon the mud
Interlocutor inter
Loper, who is to find
Something between Im
Possible not to walk over Earth
To leave no name
On the golemn's forehead

Furrow

Faithlessness, or the numb, mad years, distances
which moved through me like the strange sadness of
familiar streets was why I entered what
was once someone's house and stole the five wall

fragments in Pompeii, and gave two to you,
like the attentions of lust grown over
the best intentions of desire. First July
in a new millennium when even the sun

it seemed belonged only to exits
and weeping, and impositions of bone.
It is more, the dry rot, heaped wreckage, odor drawn
up from earth and stone: blanks in the compacted

volcanic soil, plaster poured bright into spaces to find
where the populace once huddled in fear and bloom.

Pompeii

Stylus

From each dirtied thread
comes a loving manner
and no loving manner,
under perihelion, the motes
of dust stringing together
the offal of Osiris' body
cast down, the daze of notes between
the absences of blood and dust.

Chivalric

Cold syntax of lust, I guessed at you,
bloodying the skinhead's mouth after
he called his girlfriend a bitch, pushed her,
and I dropped him and walked off hero

even as she clubbed me with her purse
amid the onlookers and the thousand
lit-up condos and neon bars, like a thousand
easts flushed with morning, that hum of pulse

in the knuckles, like the salt-slick rot-wood planks'
moaning step by step toward the beach,
and in silence I neared a couple talking,
passed and left them on their blanket,
a commoner slipping by, unknown in
a brighter separateness of an own old peace.

St. Augustine

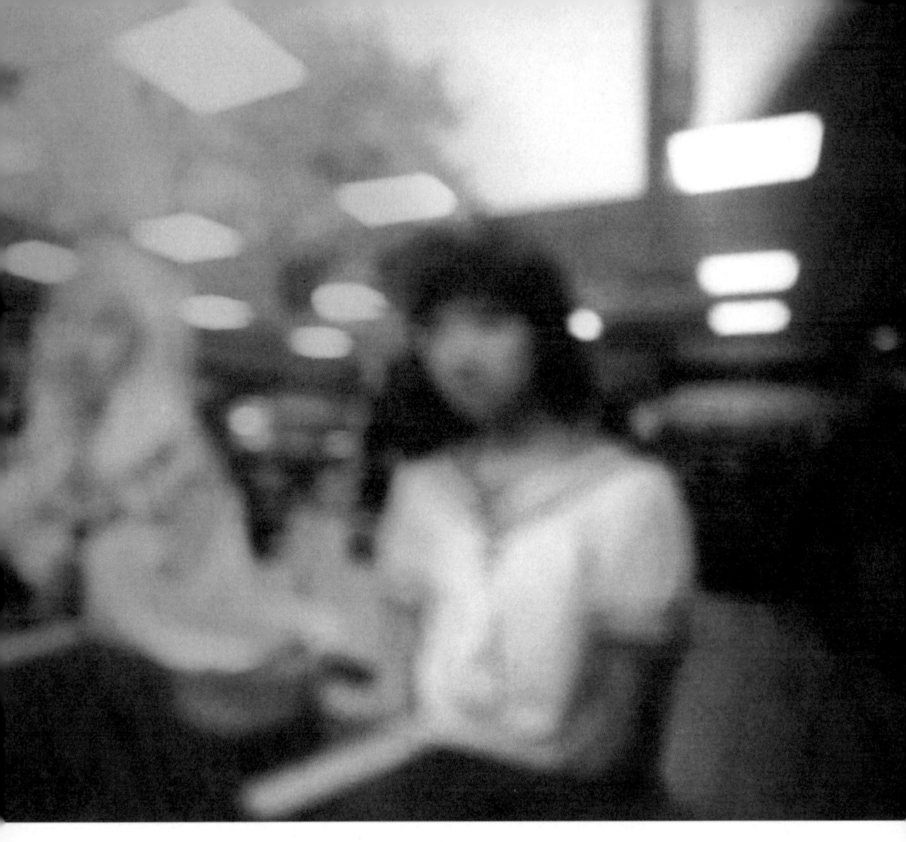

Avoid Contact with the Skin

You thought water was precious in the desert,
found every faucet dripping, every lawn green.
The cars' names resembled erectile dysfunction
medication. If the day were yours the music
would seem more the soundtrack to the life you
should be leading. Hope then that the car battery
goes dead. The manual should've read, When jumping
from a burning building aim for the garbage bin.
When possessed by devils, speak in a tongue that sounds
relatively familiar to those around you. Blink, citizen,
and open your eyes upon the rain, that bardic hominahomina.
Mortal and bewildered, there remain too many choices to channel
the light, before climate pointed the birds north then west,
before your tongue was desert, dust, address.

Desert Hot Springs

Mythos

The beauty, and the city mired in it,
lost in week-old January snow, wears
its shadows like scrimshaw, ornate chiaro
scuro. And one path left on the sidewalk,
single middled, packed by others' progress.

Because this seems to matter now.
Like the muddawbers' spent nest I cocooned in
my hand. It fell from above the portico
as I shut the door, and I turned my palm

down and returned it to the snow where it
fled down white, small and numb, as not a thing
religious, not political, but chimerical,
like a name, as glad a telling of some
one else's heaven, not to be the last.

Iowa City

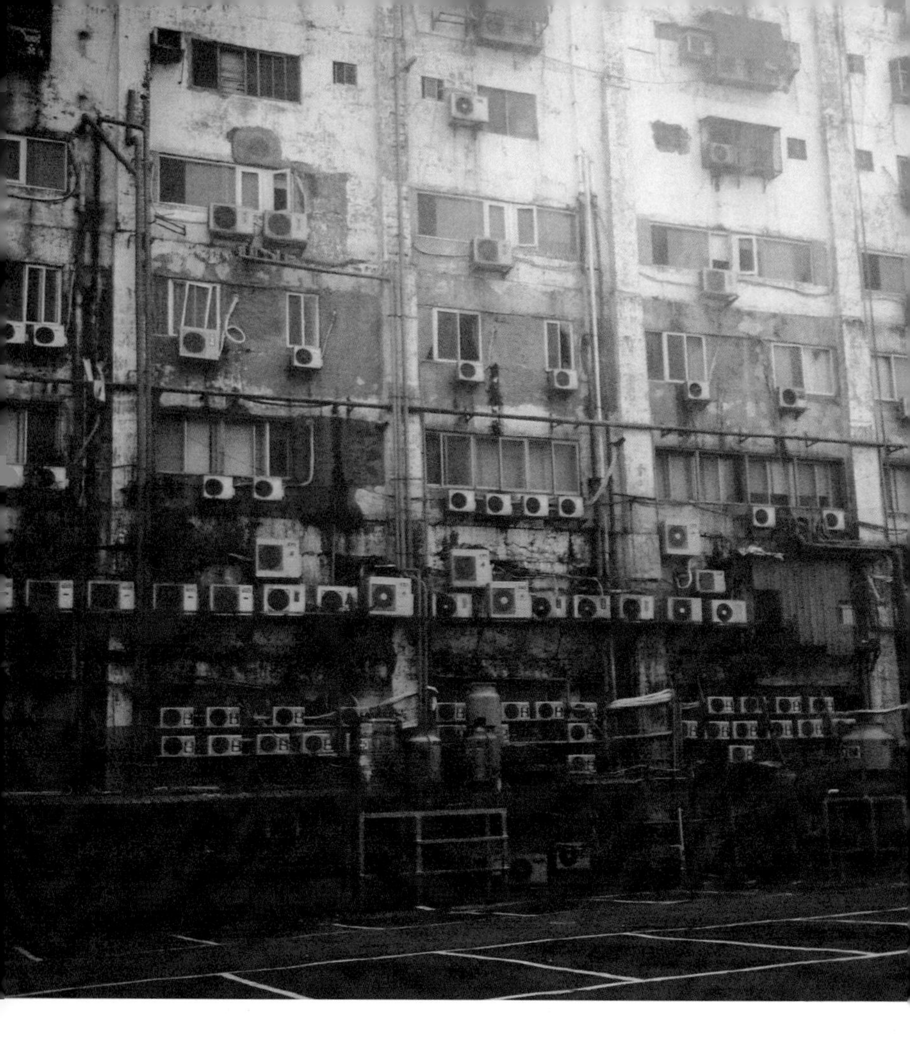

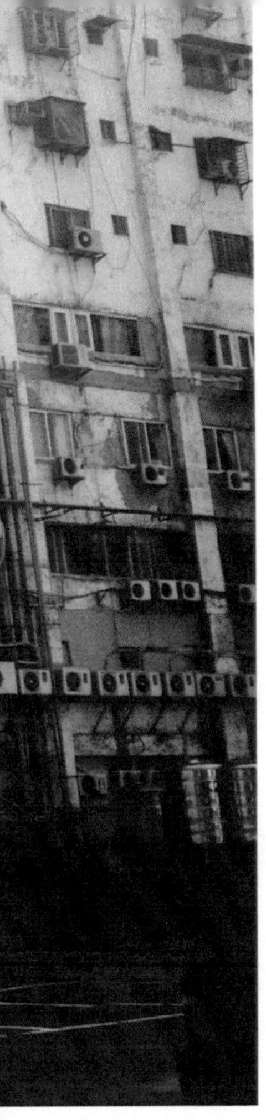

Downwind, Holocene

The dog noses some shit, tracking something
invisible and ancient on its rounds
down the empty street, pausing, bends its muzzle
to me only momently, as if to
give me a reassuring nod, and then
pads back on, loyal only to itself
and time. Let me know flesh that has no end
instead of this version, danse macabre in
the snowglobe. This, given thee, this is thy
responsibility upon waking,
this thy hammer, thine anvil, and this thy
surrender. Such manners the fly has, gently
landing on my arm, regurgitating acids
to digest my skin. I do not brush it from its meal.

Salt Lake City

Usufruct

New Mexico, your simple panorama of corrugated
metal roofs blossoming in the evening over
the poverty of what must be everyone in the state,
I was drowning in you. And on the day I shored up
and left, the man I'd given three of seven
cigarettes to gave me an eagle feather from his hat,
and said the great spirit watches over good souls,
and he was a holy man, a Navajo shaman,
and I am just this ludicrous person whose heart
is sometimes seen for what it's worth, with its holes
and threadbare mouth suckling some imagined bride,
never believing these words matter or can transform
one rock to bread or a woman, or will drain wine from the side
of a golden idol, and scare away the vulture eating my entrails
balanced on its horns.

Taos

Chivalric

Prayer is death when you offer
only the votive of your blood
to the sandfleas who make you
a common meal, monstrance of bone.
Tumult of the waystruck amid the sticklegged weal
of the sea-turtle hatchlings I found
there, spilling forth from their cordoned nests,
a troupe of pilgrims scuttling toward
the roiled ocean floors. The small globes
lighting the beach were half painted
black, to keep the hatchlings from mistaking
these for the moon, and tracking false light
away from the water. I joined them
up to my knees, arrested, afraid, fathomed.

St. Augustine

Homeostasis

Wonder, or what
to dare at, or to
believe. The fine
edges of pink-

brown leaves, damp-
ened, curl on
Fall's sidewalk, seem
foetal mice, also

curling. Endings
for it, or god,
let it end, or,
coming this far

I dare not go back

Iowa City

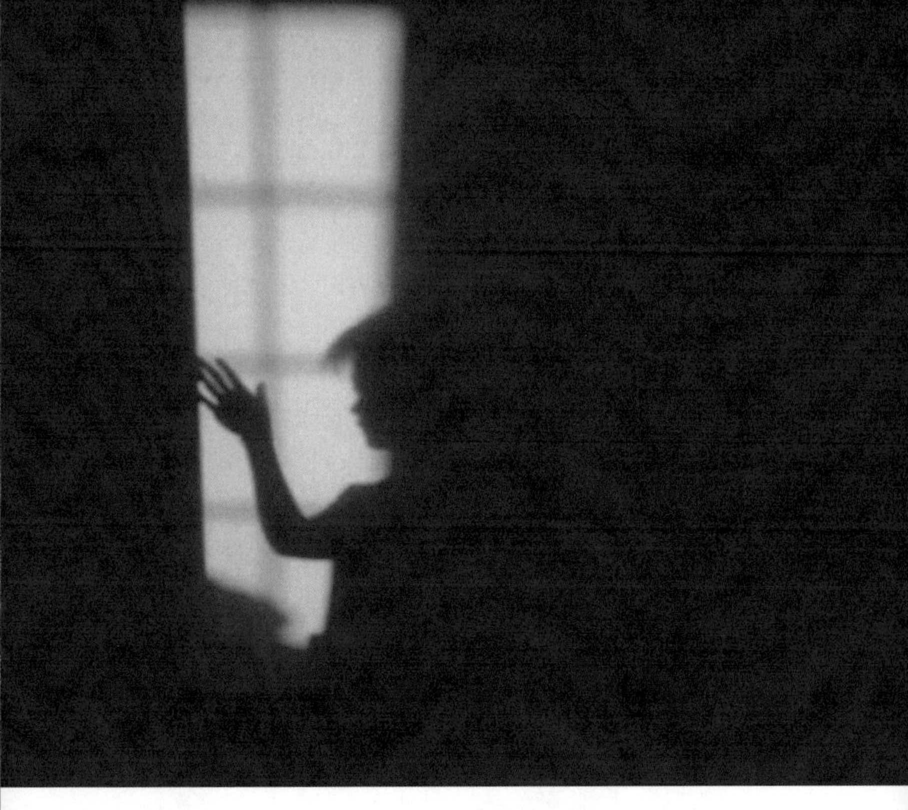

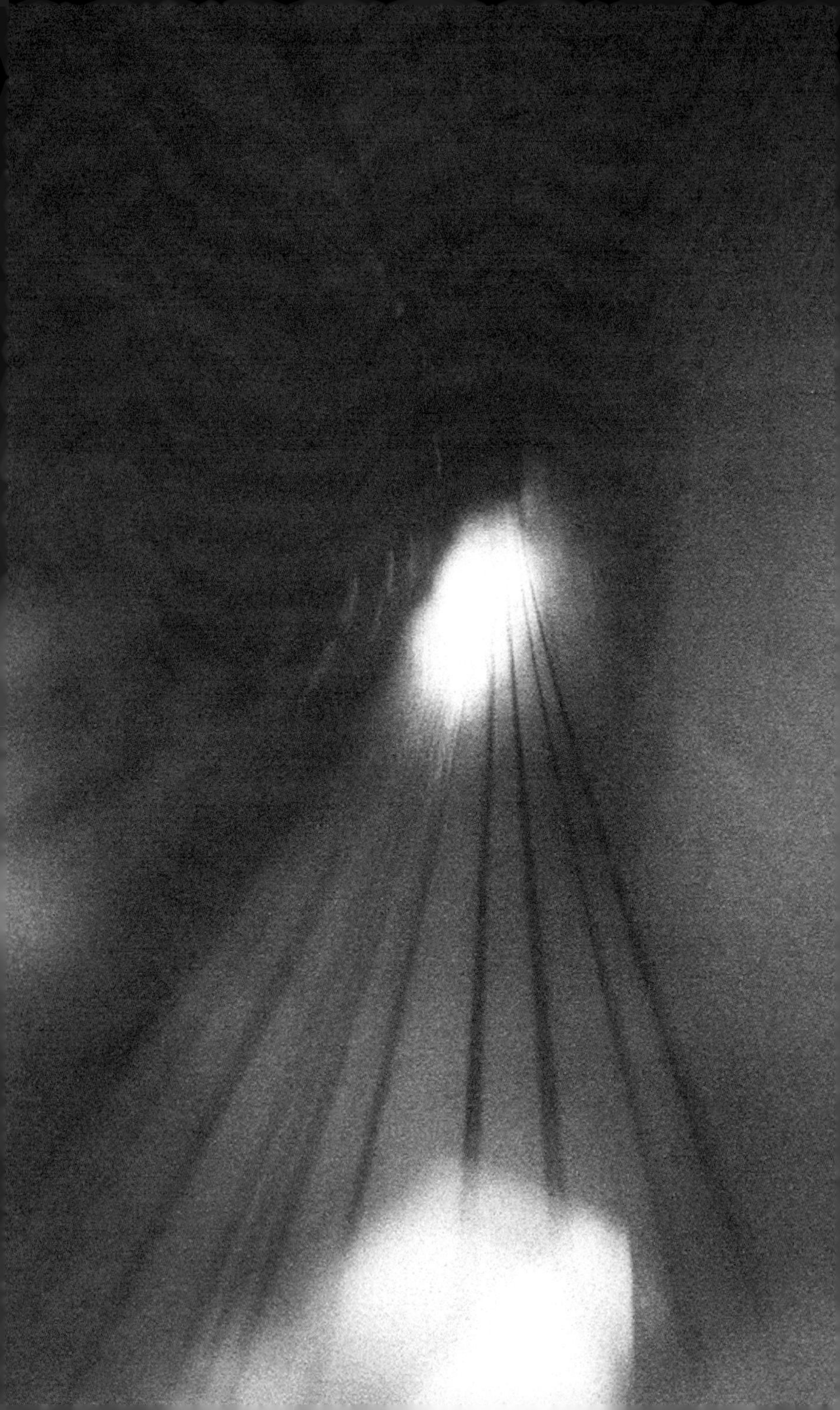

Mythos

It's good to have location, though it shrinks
in light too soft for language. Pre-dawn, west
of the river. All the dead poets of China
don't swell this terracotta landscape
an inch, throw no glaze of evening shadow

on the near-invisible willow splayed
out like a worm. These hands I accompany
to work are talking fear, empty except
a few dollar bills, and the smell of a woman,

her body last night. Down the street someone
lights a smoke, a signal like the few stars on
their tall black hill, like little hand-made lamps hung
at the entrances of tombs, there to frighten
away grave-robbers and sullen demons.

Iowa City

Demivierges

Lopsided river of dark and pious
water, my Mississippi, adorned
with the loveliest bluff houses, oblivious
to the dispossessed with our faces, scorned

and held out to you. And all that time, she says to me in the bar,
holding hands knee-high against her chalky legs
to show how high the water levels climbed,
running their banks, entering her trailer.

All that time we were trying to figure out
why. It's like the river come and waded into us.
I slide away with driftwood, hard-lucked,
within pale eddies along the plain watersheen.

Breeze in my jacket with me. I shiver slightly and cough.
It seems enough. I don't know why not.

Burlington

Stylus

And this night, exile, every knuckle bends like a penitent's
knee, scraping blanched flagstones of stars long devoured,
light traveling. This is the mind and its strange musics, that is
the wind gripping the gate vine's purple flowers, orchid-like,
ear-like they listen and fasten lines between each intent,
like the quick lines between constellations someone else
saw and named, all paralleled and running abreast
like the highway marks you travel between, lines and dashes

touching at that moment they disappear. And sadness,
I must learn it. Help me hold it out against the voices
of evenings like this one, the real things that mass
along the bank of rivers, amid mornings that arrive
like grace, regardless of these failures be grace
itself, arcady, the lower case or the blasted flower.

Desert Hot Springs

Bearbaiting

The people here request odd amounts of change
for bus tickets to places that don't exist,
press scrimshander faces to your window,
talk of narcotics and deeds for twenty dollars.

They offer fists like flowers, want you to give them
back their lives. Back from the fondling hotels,
the darkness everywhere. Their forms unfurl
in tickertape, saying, can the body pass

as they move among the streets, no sound
but their feet reading the terrain like braille,
and you know, too, the worn circles of grass,
the viciousness of passing, unfamiliar

dogs, a place never meant for one like you where
even every outdoor chair is bolted to the ground.

Desert Hot Springs

Coyotl

Were there river here,
it would never freeze.
Crow, children and wind. All
outside, and the frame of your

reference flexes to locate
instance like each was each
a light, an empty seat
more furtive than the prairie

wolf and desert. Speak
clearly of the crow, and wind,
and of the children whose faces
empty constantly like suns

into no rivers, whose just
cause was cause enough.

Desert Hot Springs

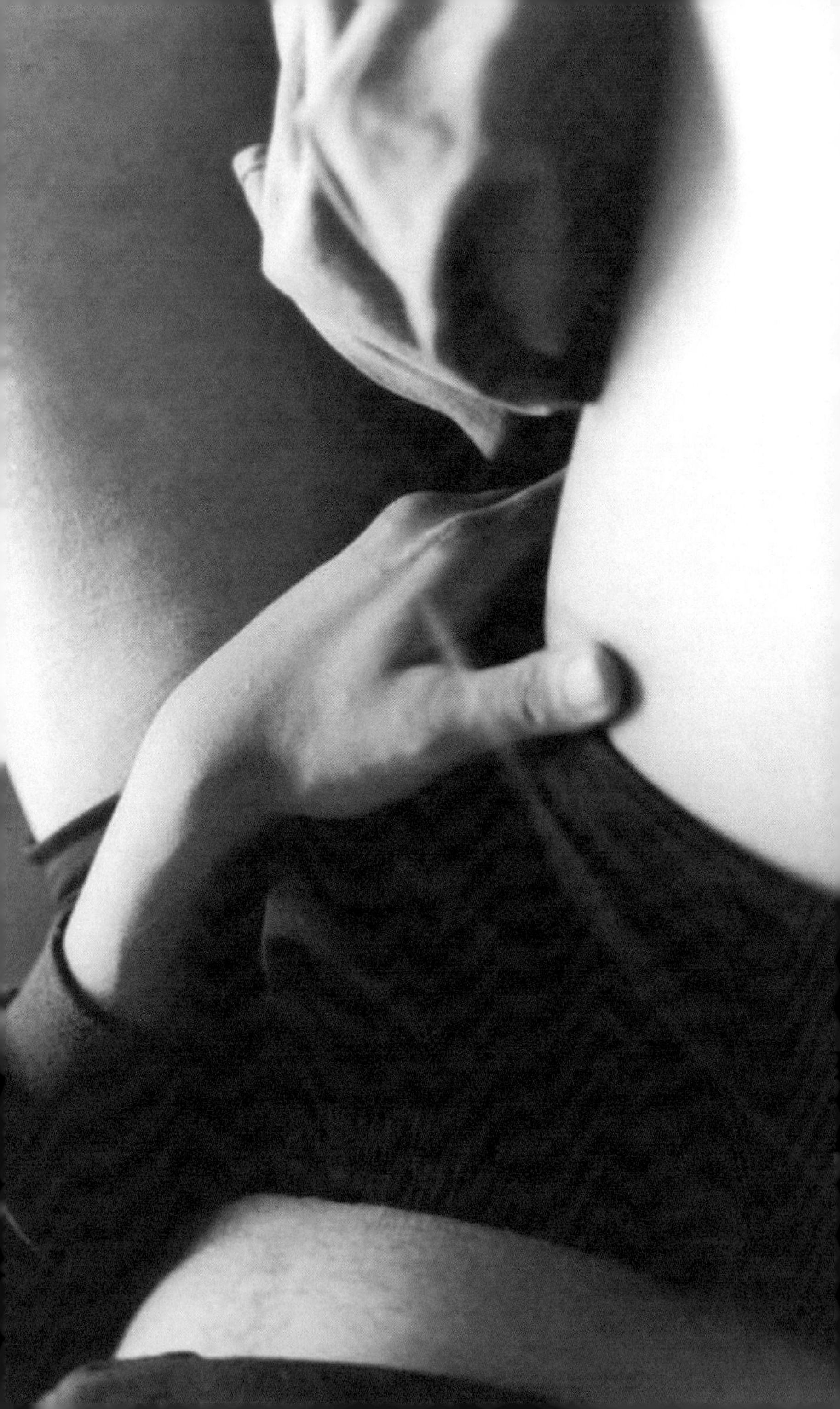

Uselessness

starving the raccoon
returned nightly to eat
my landlord's costly
blue japanese koi

in the tiny backyard pond
the mother swollen
soon to birth I watched her
shift above her shadow cast

by a citronella flame
and she was enough
for herself like me
thankfully placed

too close to the ground
to be truly noted or fall

Salt Lake City

Doppler

That I cannot blame
or forgive them, these people,
for their loneliness, faces
swimming and spent on sheets
of glass. Gonna buy me back
my Washburn 12-string
from down at the pawn
once I get me up the money.
Skin the place that lives
between scars when the earth
suddenly is too much below.
And whose scream moves
toward you, and how far
must it go to arrive?

Iowa City

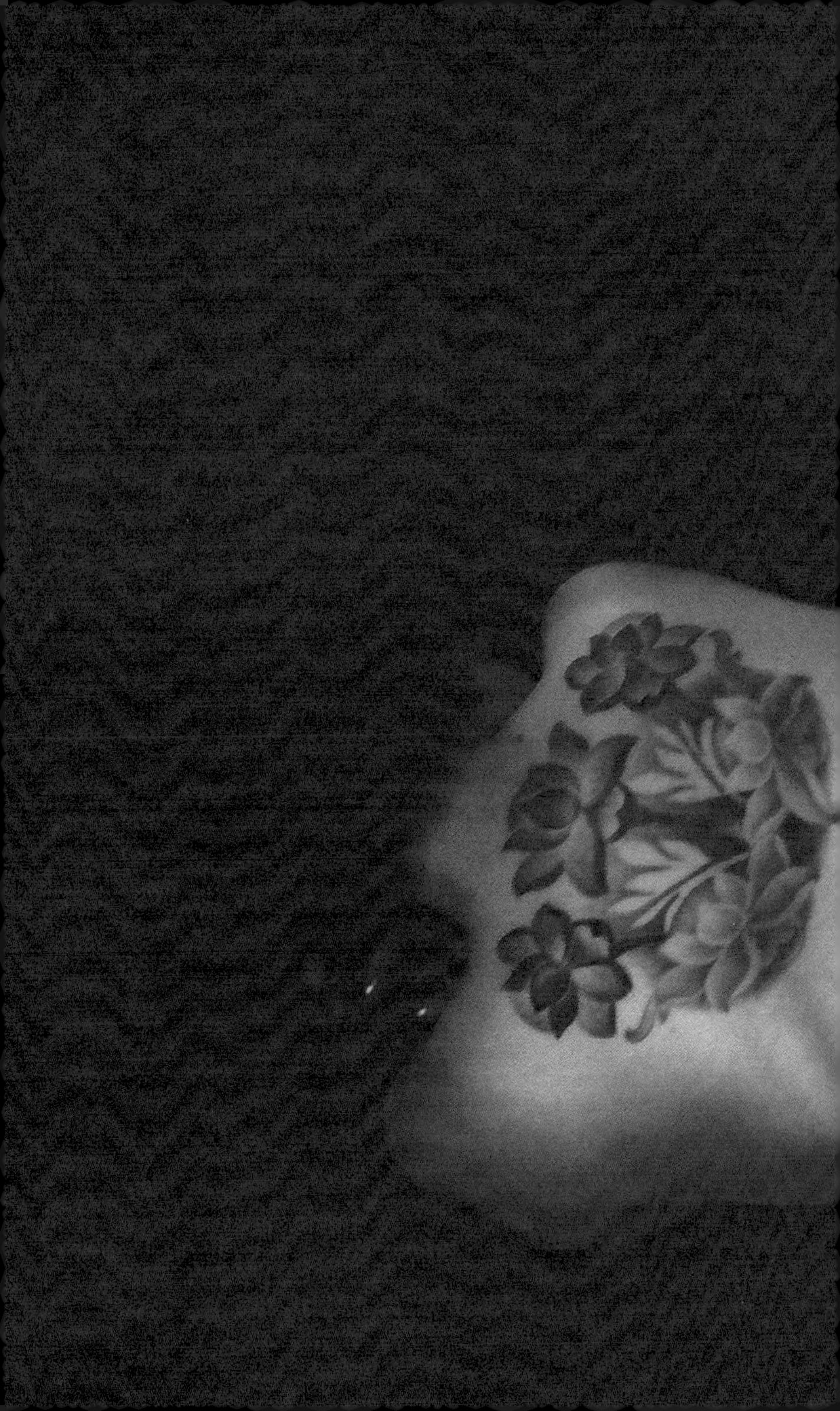

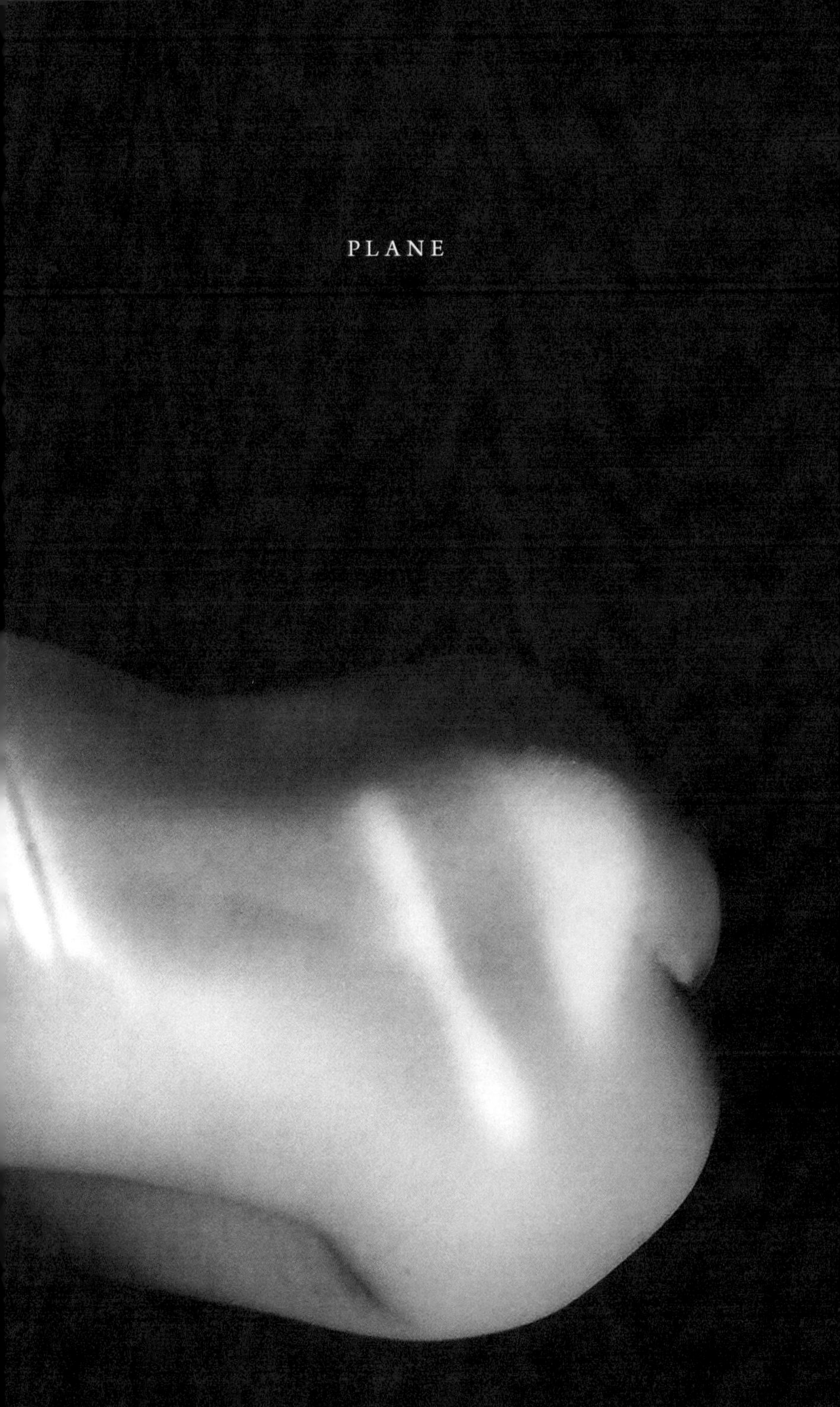
PLANE

Mythos

(The Dogon of Mali
believe they had been visited
by an alien host who gave them language
and knowledge of Sirius B's fifty year sidereal period,
star which they worship, and whose inhabitants
the Dogon are descended from, the Nommos,
fish-like men:

His body in partition/ for to feed them,/
as the universe had drunk/ of his body/
so the Nommo made men/ drink./ All life unto.

Tolo Po: (smallest seed) Dogon name for Sirius B, the first discovered white dwarf, which is invisible to the naked eye and is in binary orbit with Sirius A, the closest star to our own, and as part of Canis Major is often called the dogstar whose appearance low on the horizon in July initiates 'dogdays'. Western man only noticed Sirius B in 1862, though Sirius A had helped predict the flooding of the Nile for Egyptians. The Babylonians, too, believed they had been visited by strangers they called Oannes who rose from a craft in the Red Sea and gave them math, alphabet, laws and architecture. (as recorded by Berossus, surviving from fragments from the Greek)

Emme Ya: (sorghum female) Third and as of yet unrecorded star in the Sirius system, which of the three is unique in having a satellite. And evidence shows that the Babylonians in flight may have migrated well into Africa as far as Mali, and there may have mixed with local tribes.

Hand

There is a night searching for things to dream of, a skein
of light to dismantle and forget.
This is a day, when morning follows mornings made of stone.
The body so, in its garments
others have made. Once, during the three brief months
of part-time employment third-shift
at the train depot, some wayward man hopping a train
had lost his fingers in the hump-yard

as a boxcar door slammed shut on his hand when the engine
lurched the whole assemblage forward
during a switch. My boss had found him unconscious,
and made me go and hunt his fingers out
with a flashlight. There was a storm coming in and my boss thought
a doctor could save this man's
fingers. He was a veteran, deserved better, my foreman said,
brandishing the man's VA card.

Finally flashing in the beam of light the fingers looked like
the silvery bellies of fish washed
up from the river. They weighed nothing as I wound them
in a handkerchief and ran them
back as the ambulance waited. After work that morning my uncle
phoned to say the mare had birthed,
a colt she worked at too all night, and now slicked him with her
tongue, groomed him

in the blinding morning settling on his pair of new eyes,
legs folded beneath him in his first fist
of sleep. And would I like to come over and
see him? and I said yes.

Burlington

Expatriate

(after H.M./R.J.)

Call me what you see in lath and plaster,
in the stream. But stop, go then, sleep in your own skin,
our clayey part. But as in landlessness resides
the terrors and wonders of God, the world

is not the half. Through with this job,
obliged to keep on the vessel without reward.
Days passed, the wind in holiest vicinity.
But did you deeply speak one word, flanked

by ancient and unentered forests, in the morn,
in vain, in various silent ways, before all human hearts?
Aye, and crossed every plank from the ship's bows
in holiest vicinity, beyond all utterance,

down to hell. In full sight of the axis I did
revolve, only another orphan.

Seoul

Homeostasis

37° 8:27 37° 8:27
Wandreth, pilgrim.
Said because I know
you will. The nest
of mice in the
drowned girl's gut from
Benn's poem, be that
for me, the hatch
from which to spring
from damned instance to
damned insistence, nourished by
faith, doctored by snow,
by the wait for
37° 8:28

Burlington

Minotaur

Ask, no, say that the rain has sought us out,
    and will break as surely upon our hands,
noses, foreheads, as effortlessly as
    it does upon the nameless fleshes of the civilized world,
and will not break them. As though the parallaxed
    and inverted images were permitted then to go on
indefatigably, tendril-like, spidering into other versions
    of themselves inside each waterbead, into another world
where our hopes had been better attended, with stricter
    purity, given over, until that instant of splashing bead shattering,
to some thing more forgiving than we have been allowed.
    Their clear and rounded surfaces betray none of their panoramic
sleights flexing back on themselves as they collapse
    into mere singularity of vision, a perfect conscript sight,
and voice. The mirror and the mutability.

The barest of threads of loop and tatter at the feet of the heroic
    and the failed. The hole in the man's head
that my chemistry teacher put there for selling
    his platoon beer with ground glass in it is not more
and not less important than the rain fanning his face
    as his wife and children screamed in a language
there is no need now to translate. His face flowering
    out the back of his head is not less meaningful
than the sign behind him reading Beer in Vietnamese
    and English, by this. Mr. V told me the story
one day after class, as if talking about his family lineage
    or explaining the surface cohesion of water. Cold the distance
the mind makes. Even and unburnished the leaves droop
    on dark wet trees, and in them, too, a kind of silence. Ergo,
ergo, pia mater. Ergo, dura mater. Who then desire
    the connection dared? I am not sorry that is a small thing

to write this poem in a feckless geography, full of
    disgust and pity for myself and humanity. But I have
dug no pit, one cubit by one cubit, and have no millet,
    goat blood or milk. These I would give to the living
for their need. The mythology augments, like the dead in their rows,

like the intractable steadiness of losses we've braced
    against before they bend in their arrival. The mythology goes to shit,
was never there. Smallest things round and pompous. Round words. Yes,
    the disguises, and yes the unraveling. Yes,
the wreckage, and yes the tapestry. Yes, i am lost i am lost i am lost.
    I who assumed the heroes would escape the mazes
with a requisite grace and skill, I who never found
    the right questions at the cusp of the breaking world, and asked
nothing of the rain.

Chivalric

There is a part of the story
I would tell you, where a turtle
lives in the moon, beating
a drum he carries on his carapace
as he falls through the sky.
But it is a story of the plains,
one for timbers and pond
reeds. If the wolf eats
the heart of the turtle,
or the turtle eats its own heart,
then this thing is all of ours
regardless of who owns which oceans.

St. Augustine

Alchemy

Allow the minutiae to be
enough to say, believably, Go
back to yourself. Do not
covet the happiness of friends,

do not heed the summer's cudgel
alone. I could believe this only
now, finding the one golden
pubic hair of hers, years left, in a book

between pages 1164 and 1165,
protein augury, string of what,
antenna catching her generations.
I call it bearing witness, these gifts

from whichever other world it is
that brings love of this one.

Iowa

Finding the Marks

a friend made
in the book I
loaned her. In-
vasion a partial

love, meaning
tender participant.
Words are never
simple nor twice

the same. Each
has a name, ab-
solute in aftermath,
adding through both

tongues, for who'd believe
mine, or the nearest rhyme?

Iowa City

Mythos

As on that, that, Sept. evening, found
myself drinking with three Navajo men
who taught me crass phrases and figures, unremembered
and unpronounceable now. The night
was colorado, red. And Charles, bleareyed
drunk said When my friends get out
of prison, my Samoan friends,
I'm gonna have them
fucking kill my father
He just got out too
and I'm gonna have them
fuck my dad in the ass
I'm gonna fucking kill my father
I'll make him suck my dick, man.
But I love my country
and I'm gonna die for it
if they let me.

Salt Lake City

I'll Fly Away

Burning the pizza normally doesn't
get me thinking about death, though
it might the process of ruining something

useful, or the simple qualification
that every living thing can be reduced to carbon
and it's still nowhere close to the most abundant

element. Today, I feel it, moving through
me as the shadow of a bird might, an aspic
in the blood stream, like the story my father's uncle told me

about the frog on his mantle in a jar
of grain alcohol from the time he worked
as a miner and pocketed a few lumps of coal

to stave off the northern winter that night,
and saw later something miraculous
while stoking the fire, says, swears,

that he saw the frog leap unharmed
from one of the black chunks
burning low in the stove. I walk

to the cemetery hoping that overexposure
to the subject blurs the monologue.
All I want is a beer, a comfortable place

to sit and a paradigm shift into a world
less hands-on, less likely to burn
or turn to gold with each touch. I want

to steal this plastic lily from someone's grave
and bring it back to the apartment and say,
Here my love, I brought you this flower,

and though I stole it, it is a matter of sincerity,
of something. You can hang it above your desk.
It requires no tending. I swear it will last forever.

Scarab

Jackhammer wind, punishes
and loves the stationary
elements. Presence
is authority, only more

distant. Stone is genius.
Go and stand rooted, flesh
be shell of grass, be grass
embarrassed by the fragile

tenets gouged in skin and
stone and mud. No one seems
to live in the wind. Not here,

none, pinned, wanton, loosely
held and housed in the sap and
flutter of a new inhumanity.

Desert Hot Springs

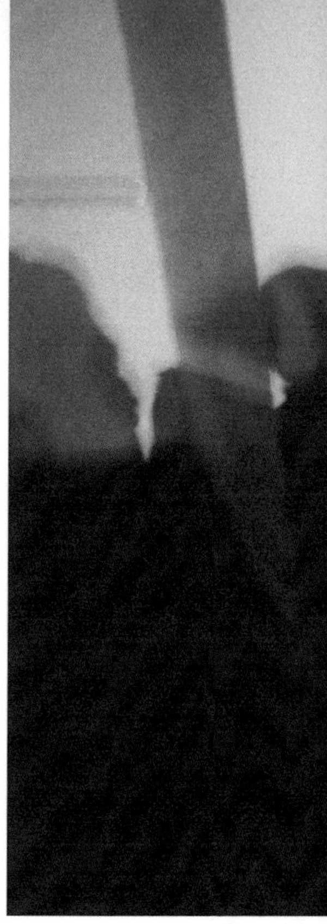

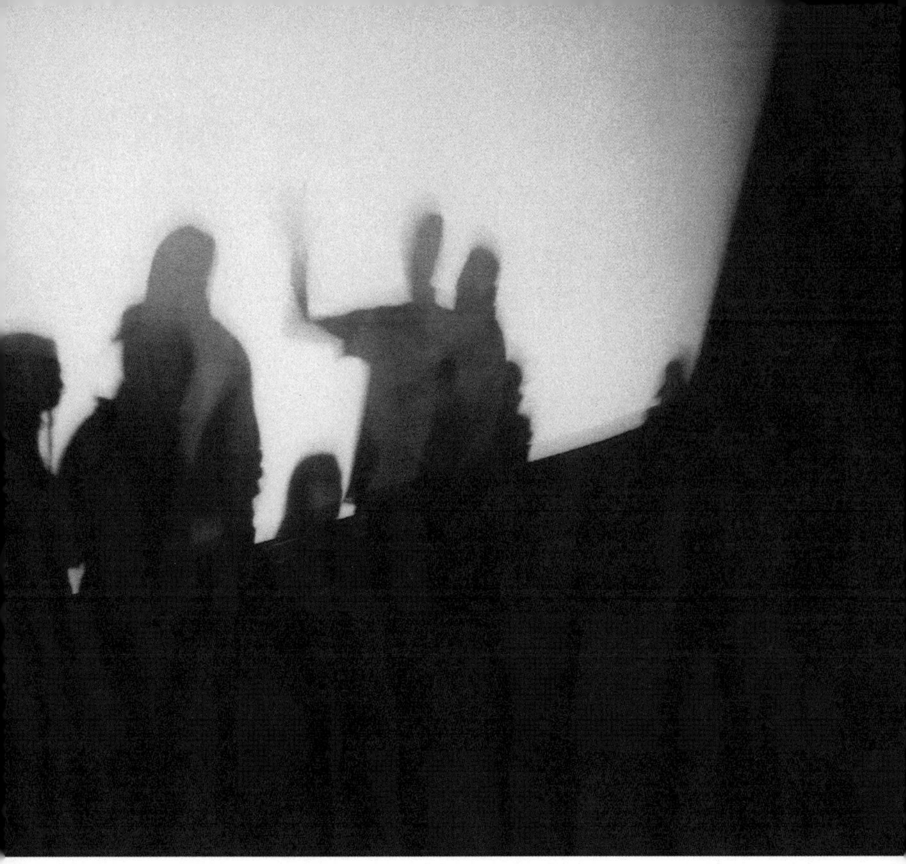

Mumble the Peg

Truman in his journal: the target will
be a purely military one. Behind
my apartment, in the alley, sparrows bathe
in the dust to rid their bodies of lice.

Their shadows, dirt, wings intertwine
like dreams of older harmonies that are not
dangerous to want to understand, but
to understand are dangerous. For a million

piles of rocks, the demarcation that the
thousands of shadows made littering the
ground, any single feather like a lathe
of air drawn on the sky's reddened weight.

Sit by me then, love, for I am sad, that I
thought I could hold them all in my hand.

Iowa

Manifest Destinies

for Parker Smathers

I put my ear to the dusk and try to hear
the Chinese words that Parker's brother wrote
on a flashcard stuck now as bookmark
in my copy of O'Hara's Collected,
the definition reading, Death during sexual intercourse
with a woman. I live in the Utah desert. A place that always seems
about ready to ripen or bloom and doesn't.
My landlord's dogs circle the yard dressed as bikers,
debutantes, for Halloween. He smiles and flirts,
talks best times to plant roses. There is the dirge, and
there is a recklessness beneath each untouchable pity and forfeit.
Would that Parker were here to finish this bottle of port. Would
that California would drop once and for all into the sea,
so we'd be that much closer to the shore.

Salt Lake City

Tenderness

No reconciliation in the patiences.
Rain slips encyclical down to pavement
is all. An historical interval stunts
on the windshield. Momently, look at Hokusai's

hundred Fujis, the leaf suspended in traceries
of the ornate spider's stilled web, tethered
to sky, to a winter that has already failed
everyone, though what would we ask of these slow

permutations, motions of survival and tenderness.
What ask the middle ground of the heart's grey,
sheer speed of ruin, and there are a few that I would
ask for. A quick world swum with light, slicked

as though by a dark oil, small hungers, tenderness,
pooled in the black center of any eye.

Iowa City

Stylus

The simplest sun falls into the grey water,
immolated and dancing, of an ocean
I have never seen making an apogee I
would like my life to have been. Cities

are constellations run through with concrete,
as they too fall amid the bleeding car alarms
from the empty lots of the churches
of the time from the time before. Let

the living name the price of clay. Too
easily night asserts itself through the bare branches
scoring the sky like seiners' nets, dragging this low
over the earth with no indication

of whom they are looking for, or why, or
for how long this will go on.

Desert Hot Springs

Mythos

Too much engendered, too
much expended. Being told so

will not do to master Golgotha from the dead
seed, to wake the word and instruct

those in beds plied with movement, to divorcements
in geography, or the coins glued over the eyes.

There is a woman I will never
make love to again, and why try to explain it

when a beautiful new neighbor has moved in
eight feet away from my door,

and she brought a terracotta army of pots
filled with plants, and some small

African violets. Why ask of the momentary a justification
when these things are enough, or ought to be?

Iowa City

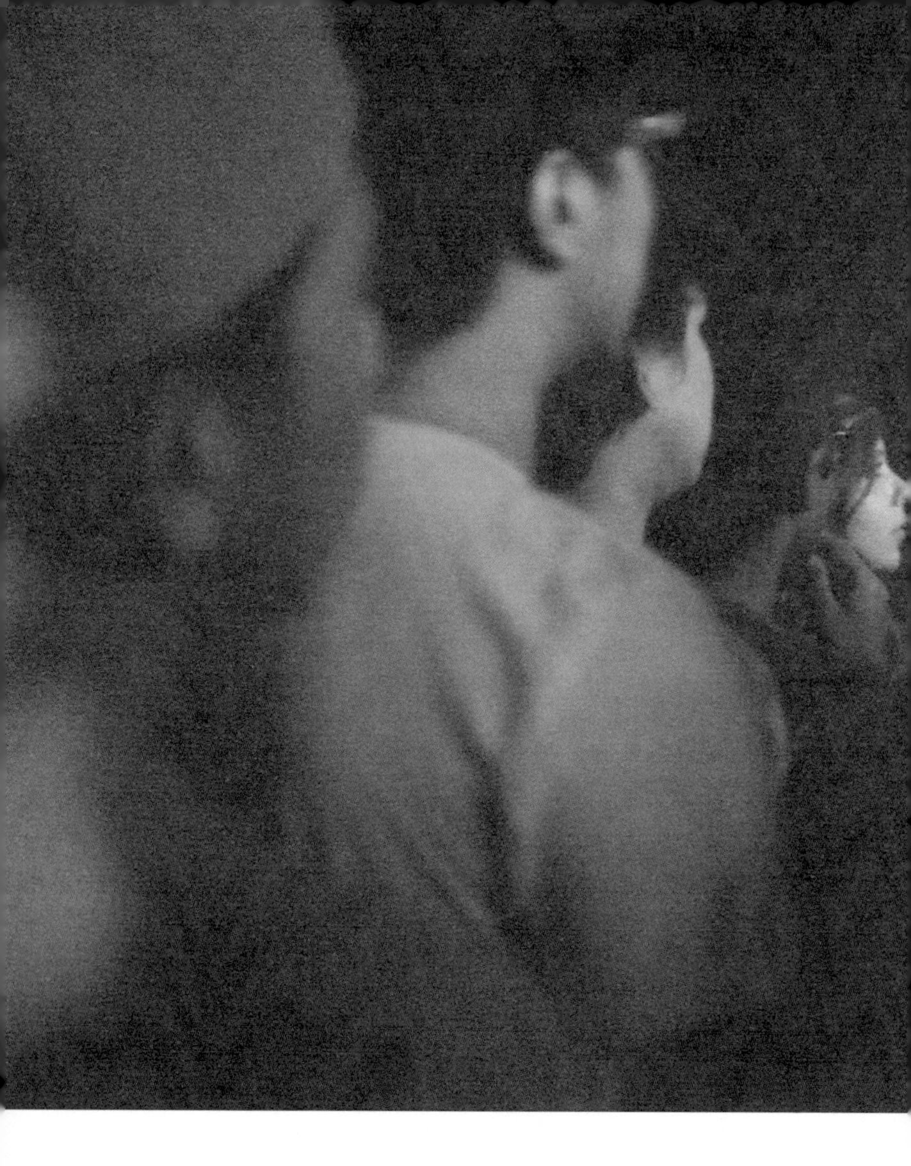

Usurious

Banker's hands, behind bullet-proof glass, shine,
like Michelangelo's virgin, dead
son upon her radiant lap, amid dimes
that drop like vertebrae from the glowering head
of a heathen god with tawny plaits,
shaking out these bright painted emblems
cut loose like mineral spirits dousing the spirit gum
holding up the last shreds of credit and phlegm
from my payroll check, signed and dated,
endorsed with what I used to call my name
before his waxy hands made love to my cash,
before the forced face of skin that met me when I woke,
when everything the rain touched made it feel like ash,
before I was the feeding tube in the morning's throat.

Desert Hot Springs

Goodman Delver

Spade churn, generator's drawl,
low light, grasssmell, pine roots like worms,
foetid sibilants. To sunder earth

is to whisky the breath with rot,
the scratch is turf and clay
opening above another sky.

I wanted not to fear the dead.
Dale didn't fear them
as we moved dirt in the small

cemetery for the single
week of my employment,
and drank cheap scotch, and sipped

chicory coffee. But it was not
reality even to find a voice
there, the one that admits,

emits, omits the commonest filaments,
words like wife, loss, child, love.
Words worth as much as a notch

in the wind's spine, piled into
plain holes, plugged with tongue
loll and click, words never confronted

by, never confused by the terror
of their inability to survive
the impermanence of the momentary

gestures: handshake, waking, work,
taste. All is smoke shining. All
a human rub yet unrecognized.

But we were, Goodman Delver and I,
able to fill ourselves with all manner
of delicateness and truth, beneath

the brief quiet of a hangnail moon,
and were wholly incapable of hiding
its passing. The endings are easy enough.

This one, like the night, ends:
the opening is outward, against
whom i shall lay my ear to the ground to

Chivalric

In flight and in return there are the heads
of the damned just below the water's tread,
bodies thrashing near the shore as if a bark
grew near to grasp the side of. Cleft in parts,
barnacled in parts, the commonest filaments
threading the ragged, slippery rock between the joints
of the water swaying like an ache and what it does
to shore is sing, and grieves us in its flow.
Of 27 bones in the hand I didn't break one
when I hit the skinhead. I can live with those odds,
which leaves me wondering how not to believe the proof
of the angelic, the backlit poses of the elderly and youths
caught in the dawn, swaying with their metal detectors,
how not to believe in their broken smiles, strings of dirty words

St. Augustine

Loki

look, earth fills earth
imperfectly   and leaves these:

a cipher miscued, a tree
shook with angels, a rotting

tooth   and is how the dead
are carried, with chord, branch,

and a swallow's wing when
diving quick and then

breaking back up, the arc
and flight making with a body's

swiftness and appurtenance
an instance and a deception,

an aphasia of such grace
we thought it was our lives

Whisky Stick

As if I wanted to live even and simply,
and to be recognized for this, and in spite of this
for the words to be simple, and death, too,

to be that, but not mine yet. This is not to mention
that the place here, and my place in it, began to feel,
well, smaller because of it, because it's no

way to live. And the fact of the matter
is that the breath leaves the body and
yet returns, aloof and sunk, fragments

of a diadem. The year's been colder than most, more
hard won already. Even so, I am not jealous
of not having much to say about myself,

having lost nothing, gained much less.
How about a funny story? Do you feel sad?
Yes, I feel sad. Don't tell me about it.

O little one, there's always
the level ground to walk, if you want,
even if you do not want. What do you want?

In the mind there is no world, no snow to lie
delicately down in, just a few lonely obscenities, but you
already knew that. Tomorrow, I think,

things will be clearer, scoured, and there will
still be these words, be the dark and light, braided together,
these words at the center, a pocket of air dead center.

Stylus

(Not Cretan, Vandal, Philistine, Osmanlis the slave warriors,
Mamluk, Goth

but Aramaic from stone and clay, and into Persia,
Cyrus, meaning bitch's son, become our
patron, shewed mercy

upon Hebraic from ash rising into Palestine
then within living memory, now within living memory

And when there was set a tower above all else
And it was there the vision died)

as from out the crescent, the weal, the gaol
as hunger is not ironic, not death, not history
as to land hobbled, even the sun
as horn, snowflight, retreat, night is an ear
as at the sea-brink's foot
as fire, catheter, maidenfly, damselfly
as that the earth is beneath the root
as meadowsmell, clouds move through me
as the red-tailed hawk on the 77th mile marker
as again I think of her body, the border, the dark
as the night is an ear, an error just so
as in carillon, caracole, viraga, virga
as the countrysides, heavy rains, oversleeping
as from the beginning to the beginning
as it is we who do not need Vulcan and Aphrodite
who needed only heaven and earth

Baedeker

denial and light
a holding pattern's lisp
lodestar cobalt leaf

now insert the delicate
the grass and orange peel
patois of bloom

or a phantom pain but
it proved this was all enough
this appetite or thing

transaction lit from within
the skewer the vertigo the evenings
this fallout east of body

As my friend (botany student, Congan refugee) just this morning clapped my back as we stood on the sidewalk outside the bakery, and he pointed to the sparrows pecking their solitary breakfast out of someone's vomit from last night, Doo-stahn, regardez ce-la, as in, Blood of my blood, my friend, this place is enough, however much blears in the slant and flight of the reasons and the cold light and the rain to come.

This book is dedicated to

My parents, Sam, Jen, Lisa, Zach, Miles, Zoe, Kai, Zuriel, Keaton, Rory & my grandmother.

To the Korean contingent: Sora Meyberg, Sandra Linn, Wayne Stauffer, Chris Carlson, Nina Gunnell, Ryan & Hyomi Freer, Pearl Pang, Berangere Lesage, Loren Goodman, Noah Cicero & Jake Levine.

& especially to Diane Hur.

To the friends elsewhere: Matt Shindell, Parker Smathers, Sara Sowers, Margaret LeMay, Lauren Haldeman, Aaron McCollough, Willow Spring, Quincy Fuller, Taylor Matteson, Al Buhmeyer and the others I've neglected here.

To Yanyun & Jeremy. What would this hemisphere be without you?

My thanks to the publishers who have given some of my poems a chance: *Colorado Review, Gut Cult, Transom, Past Simple, 2 River, American Arts Quarterly, eratio, Word/For Word, Phantom Seed & Spork*. Versions of some of these poems first appeared in the novel *Squirrel Haus* (Roundfire Books).

To my teachers for their guidance: Donald Revell, Marvin Bell, Jim Galvin.

To David Hamilton and the Iowa Review.

& to my other families: Will & Lindsey, Neil & Tamara, Travis & Lindsay, Rob & Audrey, Gabi & Simon, Jim & Sang Yeon, Kent & Tiffany.

To Minka, Aili, Katani, Owen, Phinn, Mallory, Cameron, Olive, Sawyer,Estelle, Gabe & Hazel, my other nieces and nephews.

& thanks to Yoon Ha Kim for killing the sloths.

~

Photography: Marilyn Goh Yun Jin
Marilyn is a visual artist and photographer. After graduating, it dawned upon her that life is fleeting and it felt crucial for her to capture significant moments. Documentation through photography has since then given her the creative freedom to communicate stories of people's lives and preserve happy, memorable and bleakest times. In her belief, people age and eventually die, but pictures last forever.
www.marlsmarl.virb.com

Graphic Design: Joanne Pang
Joanne Pang is an artist and design lecturer at Lasalle College of the Arts. Her works explores concepts of memory, matter and place.
www.joannepang.com

Delere Press Llp Reg No. T11ll1061k
ISBN : 978-981-11-4172-0